GOD AMONG THE CHICKENS
AND OTHER UNEXPECTED PLACES

BY A R PARKER

God Among the Chickens

First published in Great Britain: 2015
Ann R. Parker has asserted her right under the Copyright,
Design and Patents Act 1988 to be identified as the author
of this work ©2015

ISBN 978-0-956 6046-6-8

This book is sold subject to the condition that it shall not, by way
of trade or otherwise, be lent, re-sold, hired out, or otherwise
circulated without the author's and publisher's consent in any
form of binding or cover other than that in which it is published
and without a similar condition being imposed on the
subsequent purchaser.

Cover Design and illustration: Graham Parker
Printed by Moorleys Print & Publishing, Ilkeston

GOD AMONG THE CHICKENS
AND OTHER UNEXPECTED PLACES

ALSO BY A R PARKER

Monologues based on Bible stories:
The Seventy Second and other Followers

Poetry Collections:
Aspire
The Gasman Dances
Processing the Squirrel
A CARM Experience

Roundabout the Gloria
(With Cynthia Keeping, Robert Cockcroft and Peter Day)

Forthcoming:
Seasons and Sanctuaries

Copies may be obtained from annrparker.books@gmail.com

Acknowledgements

My thanks to all those friends who have corrected, clarified and inserted commas for me. In particular to Graham Parker for another excellent cover and for turning the Word doc to print ready.

Contents

Introduction	11
Spare Notes	13
A Tale of a Tree	23
The Glass Box	27
God Among the Chickens	37
The Lake	45
The House of God	49
Experiencing Lazarus	57
The Glass Ship	65

Introduction

Winnie the Pooh, speaking about his poetry to his friend, Rabbit, said, 'It isn't brain you know, but it comes to me sometimes.' The stories in this collection are those that came to me sometimes: in churches, at a convent or at a retreat house.

I hope the humour prevents these stories from being too old fashioned and fey. However, I am aware that so many modern stories do not end with happy conclusions, but with discoveries about wicked ancestors and the shocks these bring to the characters. Surely everybody's lives can't have such dire skeletons in their cupboards?

These stories are about unreasonable, slightly fantastic worlds which can't possibly happen – but I hope readers will like to think that they could.

Ann R Parker

Spare Notes

While they were all quietly praying, Maisie looked up and saw a sunbeam from the clerestory window unrolling yards of light, straight on to the pew in front. Without thinking she reached out and with one tweak she had caught hold of it, rolled it up like a bandage and had slipped it into her pocket before the intercessor had got as far as praying for the Queen.

As it fell from the wall it brushed weightlessly past Sylvia Endersby from the bookshop, who shook her head a little and brushed the side of her face with her hand, as if half conscious of a straying hair. But she never opened her eyes.

Maisie closed hers. 'Lord, in your mercy – hear our prayer.'

As if in a conspiracy between Maisie and God – or perhaps between God and Maisie – the sun was now behind a cloud. There were no sunbeams to act as ladders for dust motes. There was no opportunity for anyone to notice one missing. By the time the sun was out again it was shining through all south-facing windows equally. There were no absences. Such are the ways of light.

Maisie wondered how long her own beam would keep, wrapped up in the darkness of her pocket. She felt inside it tentatively. A touch of silk met her fingers. She smiled, reassured, and stood up with everyone else to sing, 'Glorious Things of Thee are Spoken.'

'You're not going again are you?' said her husband, from behind the Sunday paper.
' I thought I would tonight,' she said to the back page.
'Religious mania,' came the reply from the centre pages. The paper rustled to express its agreement with its reader.

Maisie left.

Will you be long? Mind how you go. Is everything all right? She heard the words he might have said.
But he had not said any of them. She caught the bus and sat with her hand in her pocket, clutching the coiled sunbeam.

Evensong. Dark and red. The church nearly empty. A small candle glowing beneath the cross on the High Altar. The stones of the church building, encircling like arms, glowed steadily from hidden lighting in the gallery.

At one point in the service Maisie thought she saw steam coming from the organ pipes and was certain she could smell fried bacon. It must be coming in from a shop outside. And the steam would be from the urn for after-service coffee. She glanced at it to make certain. It wasn't. The urn, not situated near the organ, hissed quietly, like a steam engine falling asleep. Steam did not come out of it.
'The second lesson is from . . .'

'O Lord open thou our lips . . .'
No. No steam. All decent and in order.

Afterwards, after coffee, when nearly everyone had gone, the lights were turned off except for the one by the cross and another by the coffee cups. The gallery was now in silver darkness. As Maisie watched, shafts of moonlight slid into the church where earlier she had seen sunlight.

The verger unplugged the urn and carried it to the kitchen.
It would have to be now.
Cautiously at first, then more rapidly as she realized it would bear her weight, Maisie climbed the moonbeam and slipped over the side of the gallery, near to the top of the organ. And steam was coming out of it. From the largest organ pipe; and Maisie could smell bacon cooking.

Her feet crunched through what felt like dry leaves. The floor and every unused surface was covered in black, silver and transparent ellipses; centuries of music which had soared upwards and come to rest in the heights of the church. That which had been played that day shone and twinkled; bright perfect shapes from the choir and organ, less polished and some misshapen from the congregation. With age, less recent music had become tissue thin, almost a ghost of itself. Then it merged into the very structure of the church, so that all those who entered said, 'It feels right in here.'

Behind the organ pipes a wood lined room, low ceilinged, one ancient round window at waist height, glass too thick to see through. Opposite, a soft deep light was coming in to the room from the light under the cross down in the chancel; which was odd as the room was not in its direct line, and if it had been the light should have dispersed before reaching it. But light there was, and a wooden work top and an impression of someone standing beside it. As if in a dream where one never questions the logic or lack of it till later, Maisie saw the person as if in darkness, although it was the lightest part of the room. Nor did she question that ,while barely visible, it was very clear that this person was making a bacon sandwich. And from bread with thick old-fashioned slices.

He turned and set the sandwich on a table in the middle of the room. Maisie sat down to eat, knowing he was smiling at her, grateful for the dim mystery surrounding him, for visibility would have made it impossible to eat a sandwich calmly, under the bright light of God. Dim awareness was enough.

Presently Maisie asked, 'Do you have a name?'

'Do you have an age?'

'Well, yes – I – I must be -. It's odd. I don't seem to have one at the moment.'

'Because you are outside time. Did you have a good journey?'

'Oh, you mean up the moonbeam?' Maisie looked a little guilty. The invisible face twinkled a little.

'I suppose I shouldn't have kept the sunbeam. You know. Not keeping manna till tomorrow?'

'Is it still in your pocket?'

Maisie felt inside. To her surprise it was still there. She brought it out and put it on the table. It felt bigger than she remembered. And she felt quite warm and began to unfasten her coat.

'Oh!'

'What's the matter?' he spoke levelly.

'I'm becoming invisible! My legs have disappeared.' She looked at her hands, still sticking out of her coat sleeves. ' I can see – and hear – and move about. But I'm no longer talking with my voice, am I?'

'No, nor hearing with just your ears.'

'Am I dead?'

'Do you feel dead?'

'No. No, I think I feel more alive every minute. But does this mean I can't get out?'

'No.'

But where's my body? What will my husband say?'

'Your body is at home asleep in front of the television. Your husband thinks nothing has changed.'

'That's true.' For a moment, as if she had stirred in her sleep, Maisie was aware of the smell of their living room, the sound of the clock, the cat curled up on her husband's lap, of his quiet snoring. Noticing that the cat was not on her lap but on her husband's, Maisie found it easy to slip back to the organ loft.

'All right?' He looked pleased to see her.

Startled, she said, 'You have blue eyes!'

They were an April sea. Space and depth more prominent than colour.

'You sound surprised.'

'I thought – shouldn't they be brown?'

'I am not restricted to racial limitations.'

'No – I suppose not.'

He pointed to the coiled sunbeam. 'Come,' he said.

Picking it up she followed him across the room, becoming aware of hissings and gurglings behind the door they were now approaching.

17

She found herself in a gloriously old-fashioned, steam-filled bathroom. Copper pipes throbbed and rattled, hot water ran from spouts half hidden overhead, into funnels directed into a geyser of almost furnace qualities. A bath on claw feet stuck out into the middle of the room, with substantial brass taps filling it with H & C.

. . . knees up to her chin, five years old, wire rack across the bath containing a chunk of brown, institutional soap and a bit of white flannel. Memories of hospital processing, brisk regulation scrub, offside arm first, face polished, no time to play, out and into striped hospital nightgown, next child in. . .
The steam forgave the wire rack. It was a modern one now. It was her grandmother's, it was no-one's, it was inoffensive. The soap became a round cake, comfortable in one's hands, smelling of sandalwood. And now she was having her back washed with a large soft sponge. Sensuality for the invisible? She was aware of her body, of the sense of touch, but it had no age. Was she a mature woman relaxing aching muscles after gardening?
A young woman preparing for an evening out? A child? There was no eroticism, only care, and whoever was washing her back was invisible in the steam.

She lay back and knew she was alone. The rumblings in the pipes had died down to an occasional knock. The steam condensed into droplets on distempered walls and frosted glass that were never part of a church. Maisie tugged the substantial verdigrised chain of the bath plug and was pleased by the wholesome gurgle spinning its way down the brass plughole and the green streaked bath. In the lights and reflections of the spinning water she thought she saw grey skins as shed by reptiles, but she knew them to be her own different ages, now outgrown.

She stepped out into a large warm white bath towel and dried herself. There was a large glass jar with a knob on its lid, full of talcum powder and a coloured powder puff. Odd to still appreciate the physical when invisible. Blues, pink, yellow – in applying this to herself Maisie became these colours, misty shades of no definite outline.

The coiled sunbeam lay on a low white bathroom chair. Maisie was certain the sunbeam was bigger every time she saw it. Shaking it out, it was now a gold cloak, soft as silk and warm as wool. It fitted like a Grecian tunic. There was no longer any need for warmth or decency but clothes were familiar and not comfortably discarded.
Back in the kitchen the shadowy figure was more visible. He seemed formed of the notes of music, but about his person they hung as if made of cloth of silver or velvet, deep blue and purple. At times it seemed as if it was a cloak, at other times as if this was his way of becoming visible rather than a garment he could put on and off as he chose. The musical fabric continued to his extremities; to curled-toed slippers and to a form of turban, showing his face rather than concealing it. And yet, his face was still in shadow.
Back on the gallery where Maisie had first arrived, the soft ellipses of music had been gathered together to make a bed. Lying down on it, Maisie had the sensation that comes with hearing anthems, without actually hearing any played. During the night, as she turned in her sleep, some of the notes around her would be disturbed enough to murmur odd trills, familiar themes, which then wafted into the air as incense.
Through the carvings of the gallery Maisie could see the light at the foot of the cross. It was like being half asleep in hospital,

watching the night nurse at her table in an otherwise darkened ward; all the reassurance, but none of the pain and anxiety of illness. Or there was the memory of students in a reference library, pools of light from lamps on each desk, rain on the windows, the library silence and the quiet of the books.

On the sill outside the church window, near her head, a pigeon fluttered and slept again, head under its wing. Where a roof beam joined the gallery a carved angel held its trumpet. Maisie wriggled further into the music and her cloak. She had thought she was going to be cold, but her bed proved snug enough. She must have been just dropping off to sleep when she fancied she saw the angel spread its wings. Then she knew herself covered in the cloak of Compline, black and silver, purple and deep blue.

A Tale of a Tree

Once upon a time a young couple were given a small shrub. They believed it to be a rose bush and happily took it home to their garden near the sea. They planted and watered their new shrub and did all they could to look after it. But the plant never grew roses. It became tall and rather scraggy, producing a few strange flowers in spring but otherwise just stood there in the rose garden, conspicuously different. It knew it was a disappointment to its owners, but it could not do what they required of it.

The years went by and presently a young man came by and saw the phoney rose bush. He said to the couple, who were now middle aged, 'That's not a rose bush, it's an apple tree! No wonder it won't grow roses. I'll take it off your hands.'

So the man took the tree away and replanted in a distant town. But the tree did not grow apples either. It drooped sadly and felt parched, for it missed the scent of the sea and the sea mist on its leaves. In spring and autumn when the rains came it loved the feel of the water through its branches. It grew then, and thought it was in its element, for it only knew of water as

rain. But the winter left it cold and bare and frozen and the summer parched it until the tree thought it would die of heat and thirst. It did not grow apples. Instead it produced a few small cherries which the man ate philosophically as better than nothing, although he had hoped for Cox's orange pippins.
Then one year a dreadful storm came. The wind blew. The greenhouse cracked, the garden flooded. People ran about distraught and the plants lay down and died.
But the cherry tree found itself alive and full of expectation. Here was rain, not only rain but puddles, water round its trunk. A whole new world. And the rain and the storm continued and the tree was blown down and swept away as the river burst its banks. For many days the tree was tossed and turned in the river, sometimes caught up in backwaters where it was thankful to rest, sometimes surging ahead once more, down rapids and along fast currents. And as it went, it said, this is the life, never noticing that in the process it had lost its branches and much of its trunk, so that it was now more of an old log than a living tree.

Eventually the log fetched up at the riverbank and lay there for some weeks collecting moss. One day the gardener came to the riverside and saw it. He thought it the very thing and carried the now hollow log to where it became a channel between the river and his garden pond. The log was happy at last. For all its life it had been a weeping cherry, and at last it had found its true element.

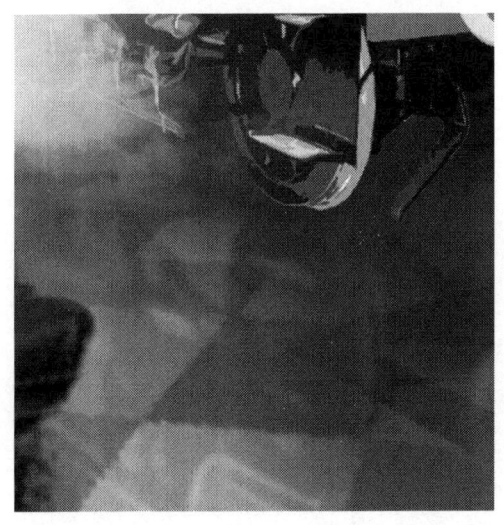

The Glass Box

On Wednesday morning the organ was wailing as with intestinal obstruction. The organist and the repairman were trying various diagnoses. Around the edge of church was a steady flutter of people coming in to prepare for coffee morning, tomorrow's morning service and to set up for Fred Jones' funeral that afternoon. People who were not part of the church crept in quietly in response to the notice on the church door; *Please respect this House of God*. They stayed for a few moments then went away again, feeling out of place among all the activity. The person making more noise than anyone was the vicar who was showing round a party of school children. All very well and it was right that they should be encouraged and taught, but need Adrian do so, so loudly? He must be thinking he was back teaching and commanding everyone's attention on Sports' Day.

Ella, who was new to the district, came in and sat down in one of the pews. The bustle saddened her but she believed she had a purpose in the church. She sat there quietly, not in a recognized hunched-up form of prayer, but with her hands in her lap and her eyes closed, most of the time. Nobody took any notice and after a time she went away again.

After the school visit, the church architect came and spoke to the vicar for about half an hour, meeting, as they thought, out of the way, in the St George's chapel, yet unaware how their voices carried in the vast open-planned space, built for acoustics long before anyone had any idea of radios and microphones. The architect knew of course, but he believed he was a quiet and restrained man and could not possibly be heard beyond two yards. When they had gone the verger (paid) and his assistants (volunteers) got the cleaner out and swept up everything nice and tidy for the funeral. By then the church was empty and Colin, the verger, with the familiarity of his job, not to mention also with God, for Colin believed that they were a pair working in close proximity, shouted down the centre aisle to Doris, who couldn't hear above the vacuum cleaner, so yelled back, 'What?' and eventually the verger got her to understand that there was a box by her feet and would she pick it up before some-one fell over it.

The box was square and seemed to be made of clear plastic, if not glass. It was transparent and quite empty. It did not seem possible to open it. Doris tried. Pandora would have been proud of her. Colin came down the aisle to see for himself.

'Someone must have left it,' he said. 'We don't have time to fiddle with it now. Stick it in the vestry. If someone asks for it we'll know where to find it.'

On Thursday Ella came to the midweek service, stayed for coffee, met some of the congregation and Moira the curate. After lunch the dean burst in like a James Robertson Justice caricature of a surgeon. An observer would have expected him to look for straight bed wheels and folded hospital corners.

Nothing strange was found on the floor that day.

On Friday Ella came again and sat in the pew as on Wednesday. As she sat down, a friend she had made the day before came and spoke to her and then sat beside her. They remained in meditative silence for half an hour.
Later that day the first of the children came for choir practice and kicked against something in the aisle. It was another transparent box, slightly larger than the previous one but softer. Flexible. There was still no way of opening it. Gary carried it up to the choir stalls. Two of his friends gathered round wanting to know what it was but then the choirmaster came in and called them to attention, so the boys put the box under the choir stalls. By the end of practice they had forgotten about it and had run off home.

On Saturday morning the local high school gave an orchestral concert, there was a wedding rehearsal in the afternoon, then an evening service for the feast of St Variable. Sunday was business as usual, three services and an afternoon christening.

On Monday Ella was back. She stayed for an hour. Her friend joined her for some of the time.

During the week two things became evident. Firstly the boxes only appeared when Ella had been in church. And secondly, each one was slightly larger. As she was leaving on Friday, Colin saw her and saw a box, by now oblong with the corners rounding and taller than previously. He called after her. 'Have you left something?'
'Oh I do hope so,' she said. But she glanced about unable to see anything unusual.

Colin strode off with it to the vestry where there should now be six others. But there were only four there and they looked rubbery, as if they were going off a bit. Or as if they were melting. Colin even looked on the floor in case he could see any water. They had not seemed to be made of ice. On the other hand...

Should the vicar know about this? Colin thought so, but Adrian was out at a meeting-for-mission afternoon in the Inner City where they were discussing communication, so he was unavailable. It seemed a strange thing to even begin to try to describe over the phone. He would wait for a suitable occasion.

At choir practice Gary noticed three squashy objects on the shelf over the robing cupboard and remembered the similar shape he had put under the choir stall last week. He shot off to fetch it but it was no longer there.

There then followed several minutes of recriminations and accusations of the mainly juvenile type, interspersed with what were intended to be calming noises from Colin and the choirmaster. Eventually the choirmaster said that as no-one was claiming the objects why didn't Gary take one of the others? This seeming good consolation he went to reach for one and found they had all vanished.

For the next three weeks the church discouraged visitors by having the central heating repaired. This meant taking up part of the floor, the putting down of dustsheets, dust and a cold building. Ella came to official services only. There were no more boxes.

But then the work was done and Ella returned, now with half a dozen other meditators. They sat quietly for nearly an hour then went away. In the aisle where they had been sitting was a box about four feet high and it was beginning to resemble the shape of the church.

The attitude of most of those employed by the church was similar to that of the white rabbit on seeing Alice's arm sticking out of a window. 'It's got no business to be there, go and take it away!'

The latest box was surprisingly heavy, although still empty. Perhaps it glowed a bit, but that might have been just fancy. Colin was unable to lift it. He told Adrian it was causing an obstruction and was a possible hazard. The two of them together couldn't lift it either.
Colin said, well perhaps it would go the way of the others if they didn't take any notice. To which Adrian asked, 'What others?' and was seriously alarmed when he heard. Why hadn't he been told? Because he was a very busy man and there hadn't been the opportunity.
Adrian strode round the church, half looking for other boxes. He did not find any. Had there been any it is likely that they would have gone the way of the others in the vestry. Should he see Ella or should he plan an exorcism? Both seemed silly. He turned on Colin.

'If that box isn't moved it will still be there on Sunday'.

'Yes,' said Colin. He had already realized that. The two men looked at each other with embarrassment. This was ridiculous.

Adrian decided to visit Ella. She was at home in a little house not far from the church, sitting in a rather dark sitting room with a cat on her knee.

Adrian, feeling very foolish, asked her if she knew anything about the appearance of certain plastic boxes in church. They seemed to be connected with her presence.

Ella said, stroking the cat, 'Oh I don't think they're plastic.'
'So you do know about them?'
'I have never seen one. But somehow I can't see God using plastic, can you? It's so artificial.'
Adrian was not going to be drawn into the theology of technology. 'I need them taken away', he said.
'Oh I don't think so,' said Ella.
' But they are in the way! Causing an obstruction! What are we going to do on Sunday?'
Ella said, 'Next time we meet for meditation, why don't you join us?'
'That sounds like an excellent idea, Ella, but unfortunately . . .' He stopped, realizing what he was about to say.
Ella continued for him, ' But you are too busy?'
Adrian sighed. 'There is an incredible lot to do.'
'I'm sure. The church is always busy. The first time I came I noticed a sign on the door asking visitors to be quiet and respect the house of God. I have thought ever since that perhaps those who live in it – who are not visitors, as I was - might be expected to do the same?'
'Ella, I don't think you realize about church upkeep, the expense of running these old buildings, of the incentive from higher authority to encourage people in, to utilize the. . .'

'Space? Fill it, you mean?'

'Well, in a sense. That's one way of putting it.'

Ella tipped the cat off her lap. ' I will put the kettle on,' she said, getting up. 'Who did you have in mind when you spoke of higher authority?'

She left the room. Adrian was glad he didn't have to answer. When she returned she brought with her a tray of tea with china cups and saucers and a teapot. She said,

'You are an energetic and enthusiastic young man. I expect you regularly do six impossible things before breakfast . . .'

'I have to . . . '

'You are also a very noisy one. Possibly you don't know this because no-one will have liked to tell you so. I suspect you carry your inner noise around inside you. It has to come out somehow.'

Adrian took a cup of tea, grateful for the occupation.

'I would like to see more people coming into the church,' Ella continued. 'Not just our church but any church. I have seen people creep in, in a variety of ways, then go away again, because there is always something happening, so they feel they had better not stay. There is a sense of interrupting a place of work. . .'

'Well, I suppose. . . '

'It is? What? A God-factory?' Ella did not sound angry, merely questioning. She continued.

'I feel – a growing number of us do - that we are greatly in need for a space for God. This is what we are called to do. I don't know how that will work out, only that I am among those who must sit and - pray, if you like the word. Create a space. I have seen no sign of any boxes or whatever you call them, but if they exist, then like all growing things, like children, they will get larger and then more awkward before they get better.'

'Is that a threat?'

'Of course not. It's a fact of life. Do you believe in life, Adrian?'

' Well, of course, the Holy Spirit. . .'

'Ah yes! The Holy Spirit! You would have recognized that if there had been loud music, large numbers, bigger committees or successful festivals. Sales and marketing! But what do you do when all you are given is stillness and space? It gets in the way, doesn't it? You said so earlier.'

'Ella, we cannot go on having greenhouses appearing in church. This nonsense has got to stop!'

'Nonsense has certainly got to stop. I am not responsible for greenhouses or whatever you call them. I have not seen any and I am not bringing them in. Perhaps you should join the meditation group and see what happens?'

'Perhaps I should,' said Adrian, without enthusiasm.

On Tuesday Adrian arrived in church, warily. He had wanted to consult with his fellow clergy but he had not done so because he knew he would sound silly. He edged into a pew behind Ella. The little group sat in silence for over half an hour. It was a long time since Adrian had done so. He meant to; it was part of his calling and his job to do so, but what with the phone, the vandals, the meetings. . . He shouldn't be here now really. There must be heaps of things he ought to be doing instead of wasting time with a bunch of batty old ladies.

He reminded himself that priests were not supposed to think like this and tried to give his mind to God.

After what seemed like five minutes some of the group began to move about and then said they were going for coffee. 'What's gone wrong?' he asked Ella. 'Why are they all going away?'

'We don't usually go on for more than 45 minutes', she told him.

Adrian glanced at his watch. Forty-five minutes had indeed passed.

'But. . .'

'I find,' said Ella, 'that the belief in sixty seconds to the minute is not true. Others have found this as well. I call it God time.'

Adrian put his hand up to his eyes. 'I feel suddenly terribly tired,' he said.

'I'm sure you do,' said Ella kindly. 'Go home and sleep. You know you will not lose time by it.'

Adrian felt unable to do anything else.

As he left the church Colin came running up to Ella. ' 'Ere!', he said. 'What's all this then?'

Ella looked about her.

'This is the biggest one yet!' shouted Colin, who being outside the space taken up by this latest box, could still see it. "What you trying to do? Fill the whole church?

This story originated after a midweek visit to an 'unpeaceful' church. It is not one of which I was ever a member.

God among the Chickens

Bessie, who was four, understood the throne of God to be the roof of the henhouse. She had been going to Sunday school for six months, so felt she was quite an old hand at Bible stories. Sometimes she went into big church as well where there were lots of people much taller than herself, so she couldn't see much. But she liked the singing and sometimes she heard words.

Her cousin Peter, being aged seven, understood much more than Bessie, but was very disappointed this morning not to have seen the railway. He had wondered where it was ever since it was mentioned in the service, but when there was no sign of it he wondered if it was only a model and they would find it in the church hall later. But there was nothing at all. He complained to his grandparents when they got home to the farm, but his grandparents said they didn't remember hearing anything about railways. Peter had insisted there was one, on a viaduct, he thought, because Mr Allen had read from the bible that 'his throne is high and lifted up and his train fills the temple'. And Peter had had this splendid vision of a Stanier engine, all black and red with gleams of polished brass work, tearing through the east wall of the church and racing up the

aisle.
Grandmother had laughed a bit, the way adults do when children misunderstand, but Grandfather had been more sympathetic and said he would draw a picture of it for Peter after lunch. He had then tried to explain the biblical meaning of 'train' and said it meant that if we could see the Throne of God it would be high and lifted up, above all of us everywhere, higher than anyone could reach, but God could still reach us.
Bessie had stood by silently, listening and looking from face to face. At the words high and lifted up she knew at once it was the hen house. The one at the top of the back field which was at the top of the hill, looking all the way down across the woods, the valley, the clustered red roofs of houses and on to the golden bay of sand around the sea. And only last week she had tried to climb on to the hen-house roof, but she had fallen off and hurt her leg, cried and alerted Grandmother who had rushed out in the middle of baking, hauled her to her feet, scolding to drive home the instructions not to do that again. It was not the place for little girls, she could have really hurt herself and look at the poor frightened chickens, and so on, as, holding firmly on to Bessie's hand, and delivering a smack on Bessie's bottom to speed her progress, Grandmother had led her back to the kitchen at a trot where she had washed Bessie's tear-stained face, hen- and-roof messed hands, anointed her grazed leg, along with comments about putting little muckworts in the bath as soon as possible and now sit there on that chair by that table till I've finished, then you can have a scone if you behave yourself.

So Bessie's tears had subsided, fading away altogether as her attention had been diverted to prizing sticky bits of dough off the kitchen table, rolling them into a grimy ball, then making shapes. So when Grandfather was telling Peter about the throne of God she knew exactly where it was. 'High' - on the top field, out of bounds - and 'lifted up' as Grandmother had done to her, and a place to think twice about getting too close.

After lunch Grandfather had painted a splendid picture of a steam engine racing into church through the East window, at an angle to show it was going fast, choir boys with their hair all on end with surprise, scattered to either side of it and the vicar running along in front wearing a guard's hat as well as his surplice and blowing a whistle. Meanwhile, the congregation, looking a little startled, remained in their pews because no-one had yet said, 'Go in peace to love and serve the Lord'.

Peter asked where the train would go when it reached the big west door. Would it wait for railway lines to be laid along the path from church? And who would be the passengers? People from another country? Those who had died years ago, back on a visit? Angels?

Bessie said it was coming right up the hill to the Highandlifted Throne, but Peter said with the patience used for the young and ignorant, 'No it isn't, the hill's too steep. It would have to go through a tunnel, wouldn't it Granddad?'

Grandfather began to explain about the little trains that make their way up mountainsides, whereupon Bessie lost interest but remained certain it would come up to the hen-house. Would the hens mind?

She asked Grandmother who was washing up. 'Do chickens go to heaven?'

'Goodness, I don't know! What a question! I suppose so. They're all God's creatures.'
That was all right then. Bessie ran up the garden path towards the back field. Her Grandmother called out. 'You're not to go out of the garden!'

Bessie made the sort of face that goes with being thwarted. She went up as far as the gate and stood on the lower rail, swinging, looking over at the throne of God, wondering about the train and glad to know the hens would be all right. And if a train wouldn't hurt them – even if it was really some sort of church train and not a proper one, Bessie couldn't see how she could do any harm either, being so much smaller. But she did not go further that day. She had lived long enough to believe that when Grandmother said no, she meant no.

She must remember to ask if Grandmother was the same as God.
As she grew up Bessie learned that the answer to that question was, no, Grandmother was a lot fiercer. Or she seemed so when Bessie was small. Three years after Grandfather had done the picture of the train bursting through the temple, he died.

Peter's parents inherited the farm. Peter was nearly ten and able to help, wanting to help carry on his grandfather's life and work. By then he had a three year old brother who had been a new baby at the time of the train picture, and a baby sister. The farmhouse was altered to give Grandmother a sitting room and bedroom near the bathroom. She seemed to sit there all day looking much smaller and sad.

At very nearly seven Bessie was taller, the hen-house smaller and more dilapidated and it was now easy to climb on to its roof. This was a major achievement in Bessie's eyes, but she no longer saw it as the Throne of God. Not as she had done when she was only little, as was her way of putting it, yet to sit there alone with that unchanging view below her, sunlit and silent while change was happening in the family, Bessie saw the stability of eternity. She could have said, 'Everything changes but God changes not', had she known the line.

She had managed to sit on the roof for some time now – right back to when she was only six and a half and no-one seemed to notice. If they did, no-one came to scold her. One day when Grandmother seemed particularly small and sad, Bessie said, 'I can sit on the hen-house roof now!' And Grandmother's eyes had flashed with their old verve as she said, 'Can you indeed! You are a naughty girl.' But then she had smiled as if she wasn't angry but almost as if she wished she could do so too. Bessie felt afraid and ran out to her aunt, Peter's mummy, who comforted her and understood when Bessie sobbed, 'Grandma's not cross with me any more.'

Almost imperceptibly Bessie spent more and more time at the farm, until she lived there permanently as her own parents went their separate ways. She was ten then, knowing what hen-houses were really for, in charge of collecting eggs, feeding and watering, while Peter, just fourteen, began his lanky teenage growth years, able to hump bales of hay about on his shoulder.

Bessie took on a Grandmotherly discipline to her younger cousins, not always with her aunt's approval. She spent part of each day sitting with Grandmother, hearing her reminisce, talking about life and death, cats and piglets. Peter taught himself to draw. He missed his grandfather terribly and tried to fill the grandfather-shaped gap in himself. He grew up to be a draughtsman, married and had children of his own. He had his grandfather's picture framed and kept it all his life.

Bessie began training as a nurse but then switched to research into blood disorders, in time lecturing medical students and speaking at conferences. She married a doctor who died in his forties, so Bessie moved back to be nearer to the Throne of God. By then the old hen-house had been replaced with a seat, which Peter had set up in memory of his grandparents. It kept the same childhood name and he and Bessie sat there whenever she visited.

They were lucky. The view remained unchanged. A few more houses were added to the red roofed clusters. Trees came and went, but, overall, eternity continued. Peter and Bessie looked back on their lives from the hill-top and understood that his train does indeed fill the temple.

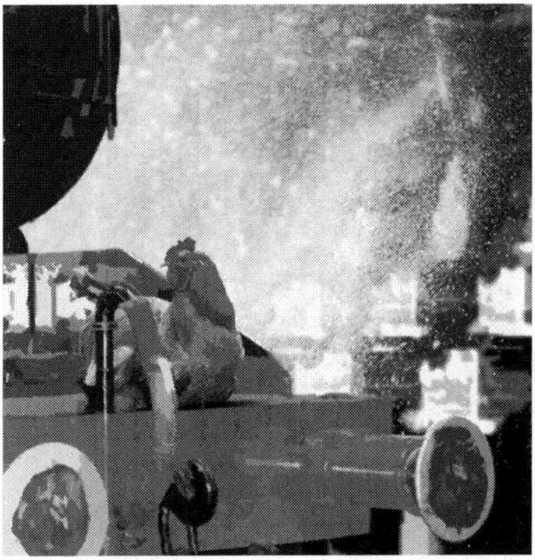

The Lake

Blue Pimpernels dazzled in the sun, wind blown, rippling, enticing you into their floral lake. Flowers of vivid blue and white, intertwined with reeds and weeds, eau-de-nil or perhaps the shade of water.

To peer down, to separate the waves of flowers with your hand, was to find that there was no end to their depth, nor any diminishment of colour. The pimpernels continued, down and down, still deeply blue, still quietly grey, smelling of falling rain. Only at their deepest were they the darkest blue. Or were they black? As if you had, for a moment, exposed an underground river and had met with its mystery. You were now complete; yet at the same time felt as if it had not been yours to find.

You found it was possible to walk on this lake of flowers. Run among them, meander through. Sometimes you sank as far as your knees before their strength and density supported you. You could sit on them as well; in them, as if in the sea, lying back, resting on the ripples made by the wind among the leaves, the petals, dreamy in their scents, secure in the knowledge that you couldn't drown for this was surely not a liquid world?

Did the lake itself invite? Drawing people towards it by its colour, its scent, and the quiet susurration of the swaying flowers? Or were you led by your own fascination with it? You had to go towards it, on to it, into it. There seemed to be no moment of decision, no choice. There must have been a time when you were an observer, a being separate from the lake, but now you were buoyant among brilliant blue waves, intertwining stems, shades of green reflections.

You could not see yourself in its depths, yet the more you looked the more you seemed to become yourself. Your mind cleared and your breathing eased as you inhaled the scent. You felt you could never survive on dry land after this. You had to stay.

There were flecks of yellow among the blue and green. At first you thought they were part of the flowers, then you realized they were people. People who had lived in the lake for so long they had shed their bodies. Now they looked like strands of light, yet they were still recognizable, perhaps more so than before. They gave a sense of direction, these light people. You felt you knew where you were and where you were going. Sometimes you also knew who you were meant to be. You followed these lights, aware now of the blue translucence overhead. The lake looked the same, yet was somehow less defined. If you tried to touch a particular flower it slid through your hand; you would see it seconds later by your elbow.

The yellow beings had another colour. Either black or white. You couldn't see it; you knew it more by intuition. The yellow-white ones glowed brightly, visionaries who knew the final consciousness. They had heard grass growing and would be

at ease with angels. The yellow-black beings had been in the darkness deep within the lake. They had endured suffering; they knew now the songs of deep within the earth, of rocks and hidden rivers.
You came to realize that these beings did not know they were lights. They thought they were still in human form, like yourself, deep among the blue flowers and the sea- green leaves.
You knew, didn't you, that you could not exist where water flowed through you and over you, brilliant blue with deep-green shadows, and a hint of something like a comet's tail, phosphorescent in the lake behind you.

A time would come, you thought, when you would have to return to the land, to the world where you belonged. You believed that to be both a possibility and a necessity. One day you would choose to swim to the shore and climb back out. But, for now, there was the dark yellow light from the depths of the lake and you were streaming after it, merging with the river's song.

The House of God

The House of God was not exactly in a wood. There were many trees round about it, but not enough to exclude the light. This house looked like a solidly built English cottage, settled in the way old buildings have of looking as if they have wriggled themselves into a comfortable cushion on their foundations. Perhaps even turning round three times, like a dog coming to rest.

God - being God - has several houses. All in the here and now, of course; it's just more usual to write in the past tense. The houses, varying in materials and architecture, are scattered all over the world, so people of different cultures can go to the one they find most comfortable. God may live in a log cabin on a mountain. Or perhaps he has a house in a tree, anywhere in the world. I think the English house is in Hampshire. I don't know why. Perhaps I'm wrong, but the county or postcode doesn't matter. You can find God without either of them.

First impressions on entering this house. A long sitting room with a settee, a fireplace, a window that lets in the light and movement of the leaves on the trees, and, at the other end of the room, a solid table. So it sounds as if it could be an ordinary house with a sitting and dining area, all polished and in good order. It wasn't. It wasn't dirty or neglected, but it was comfortably not new. The bookshelves in the recesses had books leaning on each other or falling into a space, showing that they were regularly picked up, consulted and moved about. The fireplace presented a cheerful log fire when the weather began to be cold; at other times there would be an intricate flower arrangement before the grate or a potted plant or two. And the area inside the fender was a warm and useful pen for poorly animals. An injured rabbit might sit there on a cushion, a sick hen on a blanket in a box, a cat with her new kittens.

Above the fire, the mantelpiece had more than just a top shelf. There were panels, small shelves and crannies, almost a Chinese puzzle of carpentry; very useful places for a damaged stick insect, a caterpillar or the odd chrysalis. And being God, he gave, when really necessary, space to house mice – or even spiders!

The settee was brown, large, long and squishy with years of use. People could sleep on it in comfort, grateful to all previous occupants who had moulded it to a body shape, rather than the level surface it may have had on leaving a furniture shop. If it had ever come from one.

God, in this setting, wore old tweedy clothes and looked like a middle-aged CS Lewis. He would of course look quite different to people of different ages or from different countries. He sat on the end of the settee nearest to the fire and let children sit on his knee; perhaps with a kitten on theirs. Or with a caterpillar crawling round their fingers as they asked God, what is it, why is it so small, so different? And realizing that these were questions they were also asking about themselves.

Bigger people could lie on the settee, their head in God's lap if they felt like it. Sometimes God would stroke their heads or pat their shoulders. Sometimes he would cover them with an old rug kept on the back of the sofa. It often smelt of horses or dogs; the pleasantly healthy animal smell that most of us have forgotten or, sadly, never known at all. But no-one got allergies because this was the house of God, so allergies didn't happen.

Behind the settee, which was at right angles to the fireplace, was the table, in what many people would call the dining area. But this table wasn't polished wood with a matching sideboard. It was a plain, solid piece of furniture, heavy to move. There were also one or two chairs of the sort you'd expect to find in the home of Heidi's grandfather. The cabinet, in place of the sideboard, held no fancy china, but tools, useful or interesting bits of wood and containers of screws, nails or glue. God likes to make things or put broken things back together again or make something new out of the pieces.

It's nice visiting God because you don't have to sit up straight and be quiet or not fidget or try not to say, 'Can we go now?' Children were attracted to the fireplace and the animals. Or to the work-table. They liked to have a go with the tools. Sometimes, if God thought they would be careful, he showed them how to use a chisel and to carve shapes, but mostly they were happy enough to find they could just bang two bits of wood together with a hammer and nails. God looked as though he often wished more people could be a bit more creative; think outside the box.

Older people tended to arrive tired. So did younger ones, but they were usually too interested or excited to notice at first. The tired people would flop on to the sofa and watch the light among the trees outside the window until they felt comfortably drowsy.

Then they would lie down, almost without noticing, with their heads on God's lap. And God would ask them what was wrong or what they wanted or even who they thought they were, but the people wouldn't be able to tell him. Yet being there in God's presence, perhaps under the rug as well, somehow they heard God's answers without him actually saying anything.
There were fruit trees outside, cherry, plum and apple. Their blossom filled the window in springtime and turned the room pink or apple white. Beyond were silver birch trees, ash, willows beside a stream. In the autumn the chestnut leaves added their brilliant oranges, rusts, crimsons and browns to those of the other trees, and dropped rich conkers, and all the year round their were squirrels darting across the grass, birds singing in the trees, maybe a badger; and other animals, sadly rare or forgotten now in too many parts of the world.
God is also a good cook. Well, he made bread, expertly, as if he had done it thousands of times before. There always seemed to be bread dough rising or bread baking. you could sit on a high stool in his kitchen, eating home-made cake and watch him darting about in a navy and white striped apron. You could talk about things that didn't really matter much until you found that you were really talking about things that mattered a lot, without knowing how that had happened. God would turn out bread after its first rising and knead it again in the comforting way it is to watch anyone skilful at what they're doing. He'd tell you where the cakes were and you could sit there eating apple cake made by someone who'd come yesterday, while you in turn chose what you would make to follow those. Honey scones, perhaps? Oh yes, said God. I remember them. Well, he would, wouldn't he?

He would break off bits of dough to give to visitors before putting the rest into two loaf tins.
    'What's this for?'

'Always give a bit for the children to play with. Don't you?'

'Only the bit left over. If there is any. What are you meant to do with a good bit?'

'Anything you like', says God. 'Eat it raw if you want. Plait it. Put currants on it and make a man.' (He was speaking theologically, of course.) 'Look at the piece in your hands and decide.'
A plain bread roll? A small cottage loaf? God put it into the oven. 'It'll be ready in about ten minutes. You can have it with butter, nice and hot.'

A narrow staircase led off the kitchen from one corner. Opposite that was the door to the conservatory, (like 'Mrs Tadpole's', you remember? The lady who had a big pond, full of frogs, and a conservatory with books on bird spotting, how to recognize flowers, trees, water creatures. Nice warm place, comfortably scruffy.) God's conservatory at this house has a circular cane table with seats to match, but made comfortable with cushions printed with branches of oranges and lemons. Then there were all shapes and sizes of shelves filled with every kind of plants. Indoor, bright, ornamental and exotic, outdoor plants or vegetables which, like the creatures round the fireplace were indoors to boost their size and strength or out of the cold and wind for rest and recuperation. The conservatory was always warm from sunlight, even in winter, even when it was cloudy or when the rain came shattering down on the glass roof.

And there were usually used mugs left among the plants, for God liked to take his drink with him as he wandered round, stopping to dust a leaf, deadhead a finished flower, rescue a ladybird or open a window to release a trapped bee. So he would put down his mug and forget about it. Sometimes, when he found them again there would be mould in the bottom of one or two of them, then God would take the mug outside and empty the microscopic growth on to the garden. He had a soft spot for mould for, ages and ages ago, at the beginning of what upright creatures call time, micro-organisms were the first things that God had made while he was working on Creation. He had gone on to create far more than he had expected to, as serious creators always do, his creation had all the potential to be good, but, while the plants and animals came happily to God's house, his latest beings weren't that keen to be there. He had let Humanity choose its own path of evolution, for it had seemed intelligent, so he was interested to see what would happen to a creature able to make the choice between good and evil, fear or trust, love or hatred, community or isolation. And while many of these creatures did at least try to choose what was to God the blindingly obvious right way, a surprising amount of them didn't and were causing all manner of troubles.

Sometimes people coming to God's house asked, 'How is it there's never anyone here but me? You always have time to spare when I need it.' And God's answer is, 'Didn't anyone tell you about all the omnis? You know, God is omnipresent, omnipotent and omniscient? Meaning God can be everywhere and know everything throughout all time. If you could look through time my house would resemble a hologram when it's cracked. Many repeated pictures; but a different person in each one.'
It's amazingly clever. We can't begin to imagine how it can be done, only that it is apparent that this is so and that God is truly beyond human comprehension.

The narrow stairway from the kitchen led up to a small tall bedroom, timber framed like a mediaeval hall, a roof like an old church chancel; or even like a human rib cage. Perhaps ribs had been what suggested such roofing to the original craftsmen. Lying in bed you had the fancy that the room was quietly breathing; you were within the rib cage. Your last memory as you fell asleep was that the room had turned into a boat. God was saying, 'Where would you like to go?' And you drifted off to sleep not knowing, until morning when you woke with the answer in your mind. Or perhaps reached your destination.

Experiencing Lazarus

I am seeing dark, lank creepers. Hanging down a grey wall? Or from a cliff? With a cave behind them?
An image of God appearing in them; God or Jesus? A shroud? A bound corpse? An image of redemption?
The Lord is appearing to show me who and what I am today. Bound up, reluctant to move forward, unable to move out. These creepers are to do with death and the cave is a tomb. I am not outside looking in, but inside, fearing to emerge. Who knows what's out there?

The creepers flutter and clatter; horrible things, but not dangerous. They are not binding me; that's just my perception of them; my fear.

But Jesus is bound up. He has taken on this effect until I agree to move forward, be released. He is swaddled or shrouded, half hidden under grey fabric, but not dead. Am I with him in the tomb before the Resurrection? No, he is definitely alive and I know he is looking at me as though his face is uncovered, rather than under a sort of veil.

I find myself remembering the story of the Samarian woman at the well. Why has that come in here?

I once heard a piece of music about the Resurrection which suggested that the process had taken a long time. Several hours, like giving birth. It wasn't a simple matter of an external god going 'Zap', the whole event being neat and instantaneous. Even if a physical restoration could be have happened that quickly, could one have coped with it psychologically? (It took a while for the disciples to make sense of it. I think we're still trying to.) Did Jesus take it all in, in one moment? It would seem kinder to suppose it had been a more gradual process. Resurrection must be a relief of course; in some ways. But with the entire universe across all time to choose from, why let it happen here of all places? You'd think the last place Jesus would have wanted to find his resurrected self would have been among those who had betrayed and killed him.

Perhaps this demonstrates forgiveness.

This cave isn't that dark. It's clean with white walls and a sandy floor. Somehow the darkest part is where the creepers are screening the bright daylight beyond them. There is restful light in here. Enough to see by, and Jesus is sitting on a rock, as though he has all the time in the world.

Is this redemption? He is not condemning or punishing. He is participating.

And that Samarian woman is in my mind again.
This is unnerving; he shouldn't be participating. He's God isn't he? Up there. Almighty. Judge. God in Dress Uniform. Same as your school headmistress in assembly and, at aged seven, what can get more almighty than that? We're familiar with hierarchy and

condemnation, but a God who inconveniences himself and gets his hands dirty – well, it isn't quite the thing.

But this God agreed to die on a cross. Not to sit in a safely distant government office and send thousands of young men to war to die for him. That's the human and political method.

We sit here looking at each other. Jesus seems quite comfortable. I wish there was something else to look at. I don't know what to do next.

I keep thinking about Jesus meeting the woman of Samaria, by the well. One interpretation I've heard is that she kept talking about history and religion to keep the conversation conventional, because she was afraid it wasn't going that way and she might end up confessing something or finding out something she'd rather not know about her herself. But Jesus kept the conversation going the way he wanted it.

How can another person bear one's sins?

An autocratic judge determined on a pound of flesh from someone – anyone – might not bother who the victim was as long as it was a victim. And wars include substitutionary heroes; an appeasement for a tyrant by one willing to save the life of another whose life is too important, or who is unable to bear a painful death – yet guilt is not the issue. To kill or torture a victim is nothing to do with what that victim deserves. Their guilt is the 'guilt' of being conquered. Propaganda put about by the conquerors, as the desserts of lesser mortals: the Jews, The Communists, the Indians, the 'Blacks', the gays. Women. Those taught that they're not fully human and have no right to live except as servant classes.

Is the real purpose of a Redeemer that of showing us that we do have the right to live? That we are fully human and need not repent of our existence? A Redeemer is not about bearing guilt and punishment. It's about identifying with who we are and where we are, however terrible. It's about revealing our misconceptions, our false indoctrinations. Saying, there is nothing to hold you back. There is no one excluding you. Come in.

But supposing I do, then break something or stand up in the wrong place or say something wrong or spill the gravy? And everybody else, who knows what's right, will look disapproving and go, 'ffff'. Which means, 'no, we don't want that one in here, do we?'

Are these the sort Jesus had in mind when he said 'Get away from me! I never knew you!'?

We do like our inner circles. Sometimes I feel excluded from other circles. Sometimes I form my own. It can be so difficult to include those who 'don't fit.'
But a circle is not a rigid angular shape and need not have walls. It's more of a fibonacci thing, a sequence like the arrangements of a pinecone that always allows room for expansion, and the spiral effect means there is always room for light and air for every particular segment.

I can believe Jesus recognized the fibonnacci sequence and felt a great affinity with it, even though it wouldn't have been called that 2000 years ago. (Fibonacci the mathematician lived 1170 – c. 1250). But the creator of the universe would have known and very likely arranged it on purpose. No, that's an external God image. God does know and participates in it. – Is God a spiral?

For understanding of acceptance of everyone, it's a mathematical arrangement that even allows room for those who break china. Look at a spiral in any plant and there is probably a piece missing, a segment broken off. It is less than Factory Shop Perfect, yet it gets by. It still flowers, fruits and seeds. It can still provide fruit for other creatures, nectar for bees and pollen to be taken to other flowers to fertilize their seeds. Useful and interactive – and all done without a bank balance.

It does not seem to me that Jesus came to release people from the wrath of God but to correct our image of a god of wrath and vengeance, a god that leaves us wrapped up in ourselves and binding our idea of a deity with legalities.

The Samaritan woman is saying something about 'our ancestors worshiped on this mountain, but you Jews say we must worship in Jerusalem'.

In this present situation this still, patient Jesus is disturbing me by still sitting there. Still. Refusing to be diverted. Refusing to be unbound unless I am too. Not so much refusing as demonstrating the impossibility for it to happen without my co-operation.

Oh God!

And then his bindings peel away in coils of light. The creepers are only illusions and disappear. I can move forwards, able to breath. Lighter in body and spirit, into the fascinating world of life.

Lazarus

'Lazarus, come forth!'
I bet it was raining when he did.
You never said, but tonight I feel
it must have been, just as it is now.
And the cave was high up on the hillside,
and Lazarus came out to you, and
both of you stood there inside the
cave mouth, watching rain sweep down
across the valley, smelling the fresh earth,
and noticing small twists of clouds, skimming,
turning, just below the slate grey sky.
And Lazarus would feel your hand
upon his shoulder, and know he was alive,
and how much more!

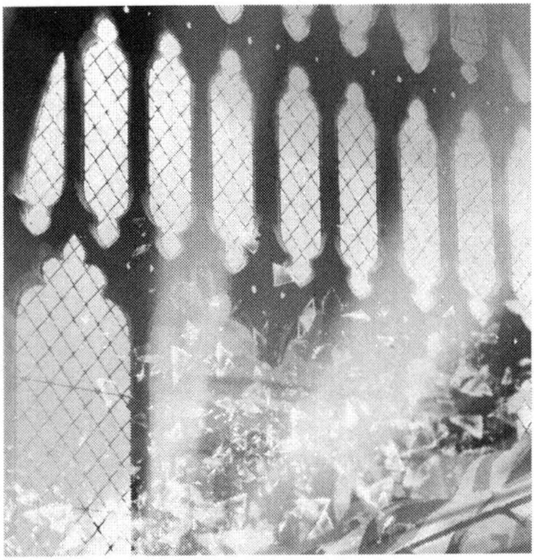

The Glass Ship

Once upon a time, many moons ago, before there were moons or tides or suns or stars and before the planets or the earth itself were formed, a ship sailed into being in an empty universe. A ship as of spun glass or mist, sailing through what was not yet air.

One might ask if, in this pre-world state, there was such a thing as mist let alone glass, but this describes both its strength and its delicacy. Made of light, perhaps? Certainly, seen in the distance, its visibility seemed due to light glinting off the glass-spun rigging or the trailing strands of mist. Seen in the distance, because, back then, distance was all there was. There were no creatures and no people; no-one to see the forming of creation.

But we know the ship was there, for all our lives, in any age, we have tried to make vessels that sail, as if, in our deepest unknown memories or in the sub-est part of our subconscious, we have known that that ship was there and that our greatest need still is to find it. And in the few remaining undistracted parts of our lives, we realize we still search for it, long to voyage on it, to be carried through life by it, knowing that this is where we truly belong.

History tells us that ships have always been built, but were we ever told that ships were also built for pleasure, for fun, apart from the competitive element? We are told of the man-made purposes of ships: to explore, to search for food, carry people and to carry cargo; ever vaster vessels of commerce or warfare, having, like the rest of the world, only a utilitarian function. Delight in ships is incidental, even suspect, and as a means of prayer or meditation, that notion is downright irresponsible.

To begin with we just know, dimly, that the ship exists and that life is about our search for it. Once accepting that this search is life's purpose, it is as though the ship begins to search for us, as if our souls are sending out signals. Then, in the middle of life as we know and believe it; during a concert, perhaps, among friends, even in a hospital waiting room, we 'see' the glass ship. Momentarily at first, as it sails towards us. Then we are aboard, unsure of the layout in this new place, yet finding ourselves at home in it.

Sometimes is seems as if this glass ship is assembling itself around us or coming into being by dawning on us. Drowsily, we come awake in it, as though regaining consciousness, waking from a healing sleep in a narrow bed, looking out at a glimpse of sea or rigging, an awareness of a helmsman in control.

Liturgy of Friendship

Familiar voices; all the intonations
of security, lull and murmur, fade out,
then create the image of a lantern,
gently swinging from a roof, above
the heads of members of the crew.
They sit around a table, planning
their next voyage, while poor old Thing
who fell and cracked his head and should
stay in his bunk, has lain there long enough,
he thinks, content to heal by listening
and absorbing essence of the liturgy
of friendship. Now he wants to be there too,
around the charts, rubbing shoulders
with the others, joining in the conversation.

Later, when his watch is sleeping,
snoring in the neighbouring bunks,
he drowses, conscious of the others
up on deck with the Commander
in control. The lantern is still swinging
gently from its central nail, throwing moving,
greying shadows on the polished pine.
A silent rhythm, at one with the lapping
of the waves and the intonations
of the liturgy of friendship.

After a hard day's work, the glass ship welcomes us back to rest at evening, perhaps in a small cabin or among friends. Now we are off duty, in convivial company, sitting round a table in the lamplight, aware of the gentle motion of the ship.

At first it is as if the other people are in different dimensions. Some are those we know. It is comfortable to see them sitting, talking, yet not disturbing to find that they don't see us. Possibly they also come and go, are also in their transition period, living in this ship, yet still in the other world 'back there.' Presently, as you recover and merge in, you take in interest in the voyage, join others round the charts upon a table, plotting where they are going- where the ship is taking us.

Finding the way round the glass ship is like early memories of being in a large building, a school, perhaps. In later years we remember the dining hall with its smells of oilcloths and meals of mince and butter beans, the area where you waited to see the Head or your first classroom. Like finding your way round a large town. We get to know small areas, then, later we make the connections. And could do so still, although we have forgotten many other routes and features. So, on the glass ship, there is a growing awareness of different areas. A sense that the small bunk in a tiny cabin is not always where you sleep; there is also a state room. Or a hammock. And sometimes an open space with deck chairs; even a terrace which appears to have a garden.

Strangely, once inside, there are solid features like tables, chairs and floorboards which are impossible to see through, as one could were it all really glass. From the ship, it is what has been 'real' life that now looks strange. If you could look back at it, you would see it like a fast motion film, everything rushing round in a blur, even the plants throwing out leaves and shoots and then berries within seconds. Conversely, it is only from our logical, rational life that the ship appears to be glass. Once on board, in the alternative reality, one accepts these things as one accepts the contradictions of a dream.

It is not all uneventful placidity. There may be times when we seem to have lost our sense of direction and are sailing blindly. Or put into harbours, the latest voyage over, a new one ahead; an unknown future. The need to call in at a chandlery providing more than oil or candles.

Fresh Supplies

And so we sailed into the harbour;
a rain swept cove of grey stone buildings
heaped around the shore. Lights yellowing
in many windows, and wood smoke
rising from the stocky chimneys.

In the warehouse, packing cases,
bustle, welcome warmth and sanctuary.
Underfoot, unmoving ground. Four
Solid walls and rainproof roof.
Corded crates of fresh supplies of Strength
and Hope. Courage wrapped in smaller parcels,
but Ambition currently in short supply,
'The last tin, Can't seem to get it
nowadays. I'm sorry. I've got a flagon
here of Vintage Insight. I'll send it over.
Will you be staying long?'

No.
Time to notice in this harbour, the little shops,
the people paralleled in what was once called
home. To yearn for their contentment,
firesides, the compactness, not believing
at this moment, that within days
this would be stifling and imprisoning.

> The masthead shows - a signpost in the rain.
> The ship is cold and wet and open;
> and infinite and bracing –
> unwelcoming enticements as we leave
> dry land, the sense of home, the harbour,
> and put to sea once more.

You could stay, so the temptation goes. Justify remaining by taking on some part-time and unnecessary job, blending in with the small and unadventurous town. To return to the ship from here seemed too much of a challenge. Yet returning to the ship was to be where you belonged, where you found life in all its fullness. And, leaving the chandlery, battling through the wind and rain, you realized you knew the difference now between working to exhaustion, driven by the belief in what one Ought To, or that relaxation which leads us to desire the good of others.

Balancing a keg of – olive oil? Endurance? Ship's grog? Concentrated Magno-faith? Lugging it out to the ship. Getting soaked. Looking forward to being back on board. Certain of the chunky crusty bread, fresh from the village bakery, to be eaten with the soup awaiting us, thick enough to hold the spoon up; it is not the weather for sloppy food on a moving ship.
The ship seems eager to be off. Is she trying to join a dance? See her weave a grand chain through the waves, skip from side to side. And sing? For out to sea again the ship has found her voice. Timbers creaking, the murmurings of rigging, and, as the wind rises, the change in the sound of the sails, from flap to wumph.

Around the table as the meal progresses, and everyone has now begun the steamed jam pudding and custard, people start retelling stories, which include expected phrases like, 'batten down the hatches' and 'tied to the mast', and you can revel in the tales and camaraderie, for here in the glass ship there is no danger of capsizing; here we only voyage in mystical dimensions, undisturbed by meteorology. 'Arrival' doesn't happen; that's linear, the end of the story. The Glass Ship is from the beginning of time, the first thoughts of the Universe. It is enough to be on board, sailing.

'A Needle in the Mind*'

'The Lord bless you and keep you',
sings across the sea when Northern
Lights are audible. Echoes
in the mind when the wind is right
and the mists have cleared. And we,
who seem to drift upon
a meaningless and endless sea,
hear that needle in the mind
swing round, caught up again
by polar magnetism,
and realign our course.

*phrase from RS Thomas

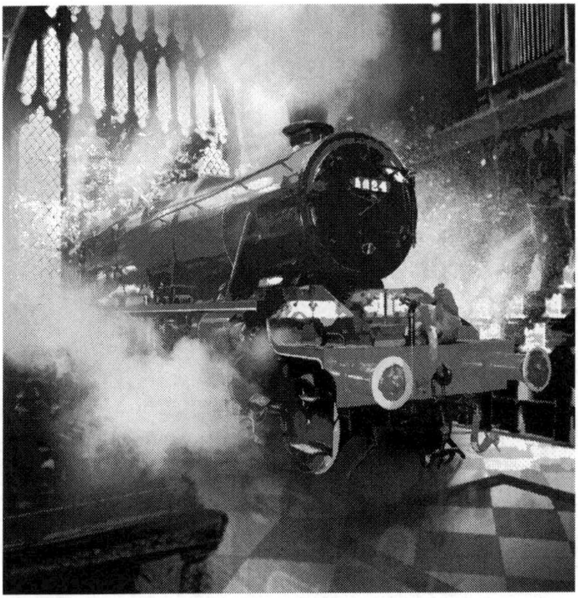

Offertory

One of the poems from the forthcoming collection
Seasons and Sanctuaries.

> Holding the Collection plate
> I find myself beside the choir
> for the last hymn. Gazing upwards
> as they sing heraldic beasts
> unto the heavens. Griffins, noble
> lions, dragons fabulous
> in Red and Gold, wonderfully
> curled of tongue and tail.
> Wingéd creatures, exotic birds - the lyre
> of course. Peacocks in full splendour,
> an aviary of vivid sound, and,
> somewhere in it all, a bird
> of paradise with nectared beak,
> anointing us with song.
> Tentatively, at the end
> I sing my feeble alleluia,
> and to this glorious array
> I add a moth.